D1602399

EVERYDAY HANDBOOKS

Everyday Handbooks (#201-300) are self-teaching books on academic subjects, skills, and hobbies. The majority of these books sell for $1.00 to $1.95. Many are available in cloth bindings at a higher price.

(This list is continued inside the back cover.)

Body-Building and Self-Defense

EVERYDAY HANDBOOKS

Body-Building
and Self-Defense

By MYLES CALLUM

B A R N E S & N O B L E , I N C . , N . Y .

PUBLISHERS • BOOKSELLERS • SINCE 1873

Contents

1. A Sound Body

Studies at Yale University, the United States' Military Academy at West Point, and the University of Illinois have proved that the physical fitness of Americans is in a state of "gradual deterioration." We are "not nearly as fit" as young people in Great Britain or Japan. In fact, many British girls are physically superior to American boys in the ten-to-thirteen age group.

Most people aren't physically fit—including a lot of athletes. A few years ago a research organization, called Sports College, made a very interesting study of 2,700 athletes engaged in all kinds of sports. Not one of them did better than 65% of his possible peak performance. Almost all were below par in strength, speed, and endurance; almost all were weak in arm and shoulder strength.

Here is an example: A physically fit person should certainly be able to do twenty-five two-hand push-ups without great strain. Yet only one in seventeen of the athletes tested could do that. Only one in seventy-four of them could do a single one-arm push-up—admittedly a much more difficult feat. Only one in eighty-two could do a single one-arm pull-up on a chinning bar. While they're not as good as they should be, the athletes obviously

7

are in better shape than the rest of us. How do *you* stack up? How many push-ups can you do? How many pull-ups? How long can you run without getting winded?

Body-building exercises and self-defense training activities probably appeal most to boys and young men from the ages of 10 to 25; but *anyone* can benefit greatly from this kind of exercise, if it is approached sensibly. At least from the viewpoint of physical fitness, the 10-to-25 group is, ironically, the group that needs this book least. In terms of strength, speed, endurance, and general fitness, the peak years are reached at 17 to 19, and the peak in physical condition continues for the next 7 to 9 years. Physically, these are your best years. This is the time to take advantage of your abundant energy and high muscle tone. Physiologically, "middle age" begins at 26. At this time your physical condition begins to gradually decline. Thus, the 30-year-old man needs physical training even more than his 15-year-old brother.

You would not be reading this book if you were not conscious of your body. Your physical appearance and your muscular growth are important to you—as they should be. You want to look well, feel well, and perform well.

You have seen and admired the excellent physiques of others— friends, athletes, weight-lifters, gymnasts—and want your own physical appearance to be as good. You want to be proud of your body, not ashamed of it or self-conscious about it. Nobody wants to be skinny, or fat; every healthy boy and adult man wants to be solid, strong, and confident.

But I hope you believe, as the Roman poet Juvenal believed, two thousand years ago, in "a sound mind in a sound body." For this is not a book for muscle-heads. The guy who is nothing but an athlete is certainly no better off than the guy who's nothing but a bookworm. Your goal, I hope, is to achieve a full and balanced life in both directions.

A great many boys and young men are dissatisfied with their

physical appearance, perhaps even embarrassed about their poor development. They lack confidence, especially in their ability to defend themselves. They may never have had a physical encounter; they may guiltily suspect that they're "cowards."

If you're not a bully, you should never have to suffer from those miserable feelings of guilt. Nobody is born a hero. Physical confidence and courage must be trained and developed.

I hope to show you how to build up your body. Even without training in self-defense, body-building will do a great deal for your physical and psychological well-being. People who are small, or at least not very strong, often enroll in judo classes because they've heard that size and strength don't necessarily matter. To a degree this is true. But you must become quite expert at any "gentle" art of self-defense before you can feel really confident.

Why should you accept weakness? You can't do much about being short, but there is plenty you can do about being weak. Learning to defend yourself is part of the answer; body-building is another part.

Maybe you're not physically unfit. You may be in excellent physical condition, active in sports, but you may be interested in doing more in the way of body-building and weight-lifting, or perhaps your primary interest is in training for self-defense.

Whatever your personal situation may be, this is a book for all boys and men who want to take pride in their physical development and develop confidence in their ability to face any situation.

This book is not intended to be an encyclopedia of body-building and self-defense techniques. There are many excellent books, both basic and advanced, on judo, scientific unarmed combat, body-building, and weight-training. This is a basic book for beginners of any age. It will take you some time to master even the simpler techniques, but they can do wonders for you. They will not make you a champion weight-lifter, ready for the Olympics; they will not qualify you for a black belt in judo. But give them a chance. Mastery of these methods—by means of regular training

9

and practice—*can* give you enough self-confidence and ability to handle almost any situation you're likely to encounter. Faithful training with weights can give you the appearance and muscular power you want.

In short, this book is not the last word; but it can be much more than just a good beginning. That's up to you. The important thing is to start *now* to master these techniques; then, if you like, you'll be ready to go on to advanced work.

The book is divided into two main sections: one on body-building, one on self-defense. The first section is arranged in order of increasing difficulty: that is, an increasing amount of physical energy is required to perform the exercises as you progress.

Illus. 1: The hip throw, a basic judo technique.

Illus. 2: The alternate press with dumbbells.

Which exercises are right for you? That will depend on what condition you're in now, and what you'd like to accomplish. If you think you're in fairly good shape, you may want to start right in on the weight-lifting work. If, for any number of personal reasons, you're not ready for that yet, you may want to concentrate

11

on the setting-up exercises. Or you may find that the next chapter is most appealing. It deals with a number of exercises that are casual, effective, and fun. It will put you in condition for more strenuous work or keep you trim even if you care to go no further in body-building.

In self-defense "difficulty" has a different meaning. It means the increasing degree of skill and practice necessary to master a technique. Although all the self-defense methods in this book are basic, considerable practice is still necessary to perfect any of them. So the section on self-defense is not arranged in any particular order. All that's required is that you and your partner *learn how to fall* before going on to the various throws.

It's possible, of course, to treat body-building and self-defense as separate activities. That's what many others have done. One fellow says, "So what if I'm not very strong? I can be good at judo!" And the other says, "So what if I don't know self-defense? Look how strong I am!"

You don't have to make a choice; you can try both. You'll go twice as far by thinking of body-building *and* self-defense as parts of a single goal: the goal of confident manhood. Each activity helps the other, and both combined help *you*. It's a tough combination to beat.

2. Muscles Can Be Fun

We've started off with a reasonable assumption: Most boys and men want to have good strong bodies. You feel better in every way when you know you're in good condition.

What does it take to get in condition? Expensive equipment? A gym? A lot of precious time? Hard work? Are you afraid of what other people might say? Would you be embarrassed to be caught lifting weights?

The facts are that body-building equipment isn't really expensive; you don't need a gym; you *do* have time; and it doesn't have to be hard work. It can be a lot of fun, whether you work by yourself or with a friend, or friends.

There are as many ways of developing your body as there are of moving your muscles. Doing exercises and calisthenics is one way; lifting weights is another. Participating in sports and athletic activities is a third. Self-defense training is yet another way—it helps you build up a strong, hard, flexible body.

But there's a fifth way to develop your body and have fun doing it. It doesn't involve setting-up exercises, or weight-lifting, or any special equipment, or regular workouts at a gym. It's the "casual" way to physical fitness. It won't give you a weight-lifter's body, but it can keep you in remarkably good shape. This method has been used and is still being used by some of the busiest,

13

best-known people in America—movie and television stars, show-business people, athletes, corporation presidents.

What's more, you don't always need "the privacy of your own room," as the ads say. You can use this method, *unnoticed,* in the middle of a crowd. You can use it in a crowded elevator. Best of all, you don't have to set aside a special amount of time.

And now, what's the secret method? It involves two things: simple muscle tension and taking advantage of brief seconds and minutes throughout the day.

Suppose you're standing on a street corner, waiting for a bus You're holding a package in your left hand; your right arm is hanging down at your side. Make a tight fist with your right hand, and tense your forearm muscle. Bend your fist in and around and up toward your elbow; feel that forearm muscle flex. Keep it flexed for about six seconds, then release it.

That simple tension exercise, repeated just once a day for a couple of months, will produce a forearm muscle as hard as a board.

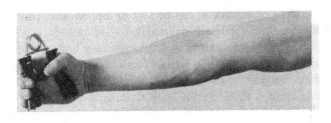

Illus. 3: Squeeze a hand-grip to develop the hand, wrist and forearm muscles.

This method of exercise is based on a new theory of muscle growth. German and American scientists and doctors have found

14

Illus. 4: The chest-expander also serves as a
biceps-builder.

that a muscle can grow at only a certain rate. And, according to
this theory, it doesn't take as much work as we used to think. If you
flex any muscle to its maximum power and contraction, and hold it
there for six seconds, once a day, the scientists say, the muscle
will grow in strength just as fast as it *can* grow.

Whether or not this method of muscle tension can ever really
replace weight-lifting is still a matter of controversy. Some
scientists say it can; endless repeating of strenuous exercise, they
say, "does not make the strength of a muscle grow any faster."
Weight-lifting, however, may make the *size* of the muscle grow
faster.

The new six-second theory is far from fully accepted in this country. But while it may or may not guarantee maximum growth, one thing is certain: it does bring an increase in muscular growth and strength.

If you're not ready or able to start a weight-lifting program, give this method a chance. Stay with it every day for a few months. Work on every muscle. Tighten your stomach for six seconds; push the abdominal muscles out as far as you can, then relax. Pull your stomach *in* for six seconds—all the way—hold it—let go. Do the same with your biceps; then with your triceps.

You flex the triceps by bringing your arms straight up in back of you as far as they can go. Or, hold a broomstick or a ruler behind your back, holding it with both hands. Now, keeping your arms

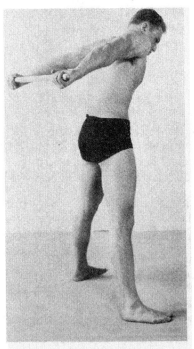

Illus. 5: Develop the triceps with a dowel or broomstick.

16

Illus. 6: Another way to strengthen back muscles.

straight, raise the stick or ruler as high as you can. Hold your arms there for six seconds—then release. If you've never done that before, you'll discover muscles you never knew you had.

The television star Hugh O'Brian (*Wyatt Earp*) uses casual muscle tension when he stands talking to someone. He presses the fist of one hand into the open palm of the other, putting tension on the muscles of both arms and shoulders. Other stars—Frankie Laine and Jane Powell, for example—also take advantage of brief seconds throughout the day. When they're sitting in their cars, waiting for traffic lights to change, they do the stomach exercises described above. Theodore Roosevelt, thin and weak as a boy, developed the habit of kneading and massaging his neck muscles during spare moments. It's a good practice to pick up; squeezing and pounding and massaging your own muscles will do a great deal to keep them firm and toned. The habit transformed Roosevelt's neck into a solid and powerful one.

Do you have to go to a gym to keep in shape? Not at all. Anybody who thinks he can't exercise because there are "no facilities around" just isn't using his imagination.

17

Illus. 7: Work out on rings to develop gymnastic ability.

When I was 14, I felt that my arms and shoulders were weak, and wanted to lift weights, but I was too self-conscious to admit it. I went down to a machine-metal shop and bought a short, 12-pound bar of steel, because it was inconspicuous and easy to hide.

I made up my own exercises, and I think I had as much fun with that steel bar as I would have had with a complete gym.

A few years later, I discovered that a friend of mine was doing the same thing. *His* "barbell" was a crankshaft from an old car. He had kept it in his bedroom for years, lifting it and working out for an hour or two every couple of days. He wasn't a husky guy— but his arms were like spring steel.

No matter where you live, you can always dig up something to throw around and lift. A bar of metal, a length of pipe—even a long-handled shovel—can serve as a light barbell when you're starting out. You may have to double or triple the number of repetitions, but you'll soon feel the weight.

Illus. 8: Exercise equipment is available at most sporting goods stores.

An old broomstick can do as much good for your hands and fingers as any training device in the world. Hold it by one end in either hand, so that it's hanging down. Then, using just your fingers and thumb, "walk down" the broomstick until your fingers have reached the other end. See how many times you can do *that* one—and then challenge your friends to try it. It's one of the best ways to develop strength in your fingers, hands, wrists, and forearms.

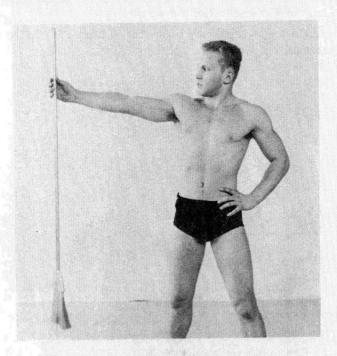

Illus. 9: Try "walking down" a broomstick with fingers and thumb.

If you're a football or soccer player and want to strengthen your neck muscles, try the pillow exercise. Place a pillow against the wall at your shoulder level, and push into it with your head from different positions. From the front, use the top of your head and forehead. Twist sideways and push with the sides of your head. Finally, turn around and push with the back of your head.

I remember reading of a college football coach who told one of his players to do that exercise. A few weeks later, the player came to him and said, "If I keep this up, I'm going to need new shirts." The coach laughed.

"Don't worry about it," he said. "Continue the exercise. I'll pay for the new shirts if you gain enough to need 'em. It's worth it." The coach finally did buy six new shirts for his athlete; the fellow increased his neck-width by two sizes.

Do you need stronger wrists or ankles? Do what the Army man does—rotation exercises. Rest your right leg on your left knee, and grasp your right ankle with your left hand. Then, describe a complete circle with your toes: first, counter-clockwise for forty rotations, then clockwise for another forty. Do the same with your left leg. But 80 a day with each ankle isn't enough—that's just four sets. You should do four sets three or four or five times a day to get real results. Does that sound like a lot? Soldiers with weak ankles did 10,000 a day!

The same kind of exercise—simple rotation—can be applied to strengthen the wrists; or you may prefer Peewee Reese's favorite exercise. Reese used to carry a rubber ball or tennis ball around with him, and squeeze it hundreds of times a day. Squeeze until your muscles are tired. Then take a 30-second break, and go at it again.

Can you climb a rope? It's a wonderful way to develop arm and shoulder strength, a strong grip, good stomach muscles. It's hard at first, then it gets easy; and when it's easy, it's fun. Keep trying every day. You don't need a gym: all you need is a good sturdy 20-foot length of rope, and a solid, live tree. The rope should be knotted securely to a branch at least 15 feet off the ground. The official height in Army and Navy guerilla training is 18 feet. If you want to get in shape for rope-climbing, practice your chinning. Learn how to lock your feet around the rope, so you can stop at

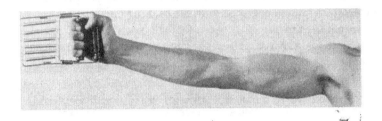

any point on the way up or down. You can come down slowly that way, so that the rope doesn't burn your hands.

And speaking of climbing—when was the last time you climbed a tree? Get your buddies outdoors, into the woods and fields. There's a world of activity waiting for you. See what the country-side looks like from 20 or 30 feet up; just make sure you can get down again.

Practice your jumping; build up the spring in your legs. Jump across streams and ditches. Jump to the side, and up in the air. Pull down a leaf from that branch that's just out of your reach—or is it? Practice your running and racing. Build up your legs and wind with dashes and cross-country jogs; try some imaginary broken-field running.

Play volleyball—it's a wonderful sport that develops and toughens your whole body. You have to be able to get up high in the air when you play the net, and spiking the ball develops good shoulders and back muscles. You have to twist and turn and bend and spring—all good for the abdominal and trunk muscles. You have to pass the ball accurately and set it up for a teammate to spike—good exercise for fingers and wrists.

If you want a sport that can be more fun (and often rougher) than football, and just as good for your leg muscles, try soccer. Anybody who thinks it's easy, just hasn't played. It's good for your breathing and wind and endurance, and the body contact takes as much courage and nerve as any sport in the world.

Work with a buddy about your own size and weight, and help each other toughen up. Indian arm- and leg-wrestling are good old standbys, and still a lot of fun. If you want to get in shape for the judo balance that's coming up later, practice the hand-pull. You and your partner clasp right hands, and stand with the outer side of your right feet touching. The object is to make the other fellow lose his balance completely, or lift his right foot off the ground, by using your wits in pushing and pulling.

Illus. 11: Compete with a partner in the hand-pull.

If you want to build up your biceps without lifting weights, try elbow-wrestling. Indoors, sit at a table, or lie prone on a rug, facing your partner. Outdoors, of course, you can lie on the grass. Clasp hands, then, resting your elbows on the table, move them together until they touch and are vertical; now try to force your partner's hand all the way down to the table or ground without moving your elbow.

One of the world's most famous body-builders did an interesting variation of this when he was a boy—and not a strong boy, at that. He got hold of a good, strong metal spring, and clamped it into a vise. Then he took a wooden dowel, or a sawed-off broomstick, and forced it down into the spring, leaving 6 or 8 inches protruding from the spring for a good grip. To build up his arms and shoulders, he practiced pushing, pulling, and bending the spring over as far as he could.

And now, I think you have the idea. Make up your own stunts. Use your imagination. Anything you do to put continued tension on a muscle is good body-building exercise. When you begin to see results, I think you'll agree that muscles can be fun.

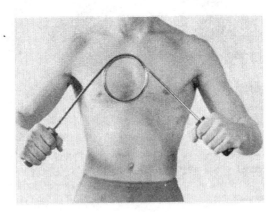

Illus. 12: A spring exerciser designed for beginners.

3. Tumbling

You may know how to do a headstand or a simple forward roll, but how about a handstand? Can you do a backward flip? A cartwheel? An Arabian somersault? These stunts are not only fun, but also wonderful exercise. Tumbling is a body-builder; it develops coordination, balance, agility, stamina—and muscle. If you become good at it, you'll be better prepared when you get to judo and the other forms of self-defense.

Tumbling is a sport all its own, of course, and this chapter describes only the basic tumbling skills—about ten of them. But if you master these, you'll be well on your way to advanced gymnastics. All you need to start with is a mat.

"If you master these" . . . it sounds easy. But don't let these brief descriptions fool you into thinking you can be an acrobat overnight. It's *not* easy. It takes time to master the basic skills— the headstands and handstands, backward and forward flips, cartwheels and handsprings.

The best way to learn, of course, is to get expert help—from an instructor or an accomplished gymnast. Most gym teachers know how to teach these basic techniques, or you might find willing instructors and classes in boys' clubs and YMCAs. If none of these facilities is available, the next best thing is to practice with a friend, or group of friends.

Forward Roll

This is the best stunt to start with. Stand erect at one end of the mat, feet together, toes pointing forward.

Swing your arms up overhead and begin to lean forward into the mat, bending your knees and shifting your weight to the balls of your feet. When your hands touch the mat, kick off with your toes and tuck your chin in toward your chest. Thus you will break the roll with the back of your neck and shoulders, and will not land on your head.

Now you "tuck"—roll your body into a tight ball. This is done by bringing your thighs up to your chest and grasping your shins as you continue rolling over and forward. Pull against your shins to help bring your body forward and up to a standing position.

That's it—the important forward roll.

To make it a forward *dive*, practice pushing off from your toes with greater momentum so that you actually get into the air, landing on shoulder and back of neck and rolling forward in the manner you've already learned. Take it easy. Don't try a running dive right after you've learned the forward roll. Try an easy dive from a standing position first, then move back a step or two and

26

(Above) Illus. 14: Kick off with
your toes in the forward roll.

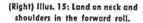

(Right) Illus. 15: Land on neck and
shoulders in the forward roll.

get a little more speed and height. *Then* you'll be ready to try a
dive from a short run, and eventually from a long run. Work up
to these things at your own rate. When you're learning, don't try
to compete with your buddies. Everyone develops differently.

Learn the tuck well, and remember it. You'll encounter it again in the following stunts; it's a basic skill in tumbling, diving, acrobatics and trampolining.

Backward Roll

Stand erect, back to the mat. Sit backwards onto the mat, keeping your hands down at your sides, so as to break the fall with your hands and hips. Roll backward by pushing off with your legs, tucking your body into a tight roll. This will throw your legs over your head.

Swing your elbows up now and set your hands onto the mat slightly back of your neck. Continue rolling over in a tight tuck until your feet land on the mat, then push up with your hands and come to a full stand.

Illus. 16: The backward roll.

Learn the backward and forward rolls thoroughly. You should be able to do them easily and smoothly, controlling your speed and movement at every point. As you'll see later, in the section on self-defense, both the forward and backward rolls are essential in learning how to fall.

28

Headstand

Kneel on the mat, with your hands flat on the mat a shoulder-width apart. Bring your knees up to balance on your arms just above your elbows, legs parallel to the mat.

Tip your body forward until your head is resting on the mat. To get the proper spacing, your head and hands should be the three points of an equal-sided triangle on the mat. Push up slowly

(Below) Illus. 17: Beginning the headstand.

(Right) Illus. 18: The headstand completed.

with your hips and legs, balancing over the tripod formed by your head and hands. Arch your back to maintain balance.

It's helpful to have a friend or instructor hold your waist until you've learned the feel of headstand balance.

Handstand

Start off the same way as in the headstand, and push your hips and legs up and forward. Reach up with your legs, toes pointed, arching your back to achieve balance.

If you find this method too difficult, use the "kick-up." Kneel on the mat, then extend your legs out straight, so that only your toes and hands are touching the mat. Shift your balance forward so that all your weight is on your hands.

Illus. 19: Starting the handstand.

Then kick up with your legs, arching your back until you gain balance. If you still have trouble—*keep practicing*. You'll get it. The handstand isn't an easy stunt to master. It takes time to get the feel of proper balance.

30

Illus. 20: The handstand completed.

Forward Handspring

A handspring is a handstand in which you don't stand. Instead of balancing on your hands, your legs continue moving in an arc over your head and you land—hopefully—back on your feet.

After a short run toward the mat, throw your hands down to the mat at shoulder's width, arms straight and hands spread for wide support.

Kick one leg up first, then swing up with the other. As your legs

31

Illus. 21: Beginning the forward handspring.

Illus. 22: Near the peak of the forward handspring.

32

continue in an arc over your head, push off with your arms, arching your body high by pushing your hips upward. This will pull your shoulders up as your legs complete the arc and you land, feet together, on the mat.

(Above) Illus. 23: Past the peak of the forward handspring.

(Below) Illus. 24: Plan to land with feet together.

33

Arabian Handspring

That's just a fancy name for a handspring you take from a dive. Instead of coming down into a forward roll, you land on your hands and arch your legs over your head, as in the regular handspring. There's not a great deal of difference between the regular and the Arabian. It's a very handsome, impressive stunt, but requires extra practice.

The Back Bend

If you learn the back bend first, you'll find it easier to learn the back flip later. Stand with your back to the mat, feet about 12 inches apart. (Later, when you've developed good flexibility in your back and mastered the stunt, you'll be able to do the back bend with your feet closer together.)

Raise your arms up over your head and bend your knees. Slowly bend backward, maintaining your balance by keeping your hips balanced over your feet. You'll find you can do this by bending your knees more.

Illus. 26: The back bend.

Continue bending backward until you can reach the mat in back of you with your hands. Have a friend hold your waist at the

Illus. 27.

start. Once you have contact, distribute your weight equally over the four points of contact—both hands and feet.

There you are—gracefully arched in a back bend. *Now* what? How do you get out of it? It isn't considered cricket to just collapse onto the mat. Learning how to recover to your feet again isn't easy, but it's the only way to do it. It takes good strong muscles all over —in your thighs, abdomen, back and arms. One way to develop these muscles, of course, is to *practice* proper recovery. Another way is to strengthen your muscles with the kinds of exercises and weight training you'll find in the following chapters.

The first step is to try to push yourself up with your hands in order to balance your weight over your feet again. Bend your knees, thrust your hips forward and tighten your abdominal and thigh muscles to pull yourself up to a standing position. Swinging your arms up forward, toward your hips, will also help. But don't expect success on the first few tries.

The Front Flip

If you want to be formal, call it a forward somersault. Around the diving board or trampoline, though, most people simply call it a front flip. If you can do a forward roll from a dive, you can learn the front flip—eventually. Some people—a few—find it easy. Most people take their time in working up to it; it may take a few weeks, or as long as six months, depending on your own personality, physical ability, and the training available.

Take a short run up to the edge of the mat, then jump down (as for a dive) on both feet for the take-off. Aim for *height*, not distance. As you spring up, tuck your body into a tight ball: bring your chin down into your chest and pull your knees up to your chest, clasping your shins.

If you get off the ground with a good spring and go into a tight tuck, you shouldn't have any trouble performing a complete somersault. Keep your legs together as you turn, then open up from the tucked position in order to drop down to your feet.

36

Illus. 28: Going into the front flip.

Illus. 29: About to land in the front flip.

Bend your knees slightly to keep your balance and cushion the landing.

37

Illus. 30: Crouching for the
back flip.

The Back Flip

It takes a while to get from the forward roll to the forward somersault, and it's an equal victory to proceed from the backward roll to the back flip. Work up to it in gradual, progressive stages, trying for a little more height each time.

From a standing position, crouch down on your toes in preparation for the upward throw. Swing your arms back, as you would before a dive, and then throw them upward as you push off straight up in the air with your legs. Throw your head back immediately. This will automatically bring your shoulders and arms up and back also. Bring your knees up into a tight tuck and continue the circular roll backwards. Open up as you come around, kicking out of the tuck with your legs. Bring your feet down and swing your arms forward for the landing.

38

Illus. 32: Feet coming over in the back flip.

Illus. 33: Landing in the back flip.

The Cartwheel

If you've ever tried a cartwheel, you know it's not easy. Yet, like all athletic performances, it looks easy if it's done well. The cartwheel most youngsters do in school, by bending forward and tumbling around from hand to foot, is not really a cartwheel at all, of course.

There's only one solution: before you try a cartwheel, learn the handstand first. That's what a good cartwheel requires, as well as the ability to whip your body sideways into and out of a handstand. Instead of bending forward, in fact, you should be using the opposite kind of arch—the regular handstand arch.

Begin the cartwheel from a short skip to the side, whipping your body sideways and down, kicking up hard with the opposite leg. The other leg follows up as both hands support your body momentarily in a handstand. Your body spins through the handstand in a sideward arc as your feet swing over and down to the ground again.

Cartwheels are beautiful when they're well done; don't be discouraged if you find they take a long time to learn and perfect.

40

Illus. 34: The cartwheel.

Continue practicing the handstand and the sideways whip, and you'll eventually master the stunt.

4. Setting-up Exercises

Many people make the mistake of starting a body-building program by lifting weights, without doing any preliminary exercises. Often they use weights that are too heavy, and then of course they become discouraged.

The first thing to remember is that you should never strain yourself with weights. You don't have to. But more about that later.

The second point is: Before you start any weight-lifting session, you should always do a series of setting-up exercises. You've probably had a taste of these calisthenics in school; they're also a regular part of the Basic Training programs in all of the Armed Forces.

It's easy—and wrong—to think that these exercises are unimportant because they're not done with weights. Setting-up exercises can keep you in good physical shape if you do them regularly—even if you never work with weights. They're not only designed to loosen, stretch, toughen, and warm up your muscles; they're also excellent body-builders in themselves. Give them half a chance and they'll keep you hard and trim.

You can do these exercises quickly, with snap and precision, after the first few sessions. In the beginning, don't work so fast that you run out of breath in a few minutes. Your motions should be smooth and rhythmic.

And don't forget to breathe. That may sound funny, but there's a natural tendency to hold your breath while exercising. You may not even be aware of it, so you should try to think about it consciously at first. Despite what you may have heard or read, there's no special way to breathe while exercising. Some people think you should breathe only through your nose. Others say, "Inhale through your nose, exhale through your mouth." And still others will tell you that athletes should breathe *only* through the mouth while exercising.

You can disregard all the special tricks. Not one of them has been "scientifically proven," as people will claim. The important thing is to breathe deeply, as often as you need, in a regular way. Breathe through your mouth whenever you need more air. Do whatever is most comfortable for you—but don't forget to breathe. It's an important part of the exercises.

Illus. 35: Knees straight in the toe-toucher.

1. TOE-TOUCHER. Stand erect, hands on hips. *Keeping knees straight*, bend from waist and touch toes (or floor) with fingertips. Try 12 repetitions.

This is excellent for the abdominal muscles; the exercise is a well-known stomach-firmer and waist-reducer. As your suppleness

43

increases, touch the floor with your palms, instead of your finger-tips.

2. SIDE-BENDER. Starting position: Stand erect, hands on hips. Bend forward at waist so that upper body is parallel to floor. Now proceed to rotate your upper body around in a loop, bending as far as you can in each direction. Do 12 repetitions—that is, 12 complete circles.

Illus. 36: Bend forward from the waist, then rotate to the back (Illus. 37).

Don't be afraid to stretch those muscles. Do the exercise in a smooth, swinging movement, without stopping or pausing. This doesn't make it easier, but harder, if you re doing the exercise right and really bending and stretching. This is an old military exercise, and still very effective. You can have strong arms and shoulders and legs, and still be weak if your trunk muscles are

44

weak. The abdominal, back, and side muscles are the foundation of a solid, powerful body. Yet these are the weakest parts of the body in most men. That's why a number of these exercises are geared to strong abdominal and trunk development.

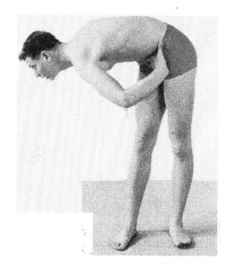

3. LEG-RAISER. In supine position (lying on back), place hands under hips, palms down on floor. Raise legs to vertical position,

Illus. 39: Keep feet together in the leg-raiser.

keeping feet together. Then lower them slowly, bringing heels to within a few inches of the floor, and hold legs in this position for four seconds. Try five repetitions for the first two weeks, then increase to 10.

You'll feel this in your abdominal muscles at first, but they'll soon toughen up. This is one of the finest exercises you can do. In just about a month it will give you a ripply, washerboard stomach, hard as a rock. The longer you can hold your legs off the floor, of course, the more you'll develop.

4. BICYCLE KICK. Lie on your back, hands at sides, palms down. Throw your legs into the air and move them in a rotating kick, as if riding a bicycle. Forming a supporting triangle, with hands on hips, elbows and arms on floor, is not good. It prevents your stomach and side muscles from getting most of the benefits of the exercise. Get your lower body up in the air as far as you can with your own trunk-power. Do 50 cycles with each leg.

After you have done this setting-up exercise for about two weeks,

regularly, your abdominal muscles will be strong enough to enable you to really kick out and kick hard. This kind of training can come in handy in a self-defense situation, since it's actually a basic jiu-jitsu technique. Just as certain wild animals fight very effectively from this position, using their feet and claws to attack and defend, and protect the stomach, so can you use it for strong kicking power if necessary. You can effectively stop the opponent who tries to jump you, and you can tangle his feet if thrown to the ground on your back.

5. SIT-UPS. Lie on back, hands at sides, feet together. Bring body to sitting position without bending knees or using hands or arms to push up. All the work is done by the abdominal and back muscles. Arms should rise slowly, roughly parallel to floor, as you sit up; do not stop when sitting position is reached, but

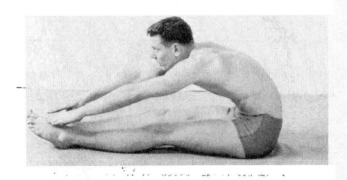

Illus. 42: The sit-up.

continue to bend forward and touch toes with fingertips. Try 12 repetitions.

6. PUSH-UPS. Start in prone position (lying on stomach). Place hands on floor, a shoulder's-width apart. Keeping back straight, push yourself up to arm's length, then lower yourself until chest or chin touches floor; then push up again. Begin with 10 repetitions, and continue to increase the number until you can do 25 or 30 push-ups in good form.

It is important to keep the body straight, for proper form: no sagging in the middle, no hunching up. All the work is done with the arms and shoulders. This is especially good for the triceps and deltoids. (See pages 57 and 58 for Muscle Chart.)

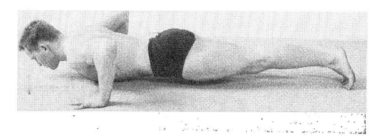

Illus. 43: The push-up, starting position.

Illus. 44: Good form in a push-up.

49

5. Should You Lift Weights?

In the second chapter, we mentioned the "six-second theory" of muscle growth. The theory may be a good one. Until it is better established and more widely accepted in this country, however, we'll have to rely on weight-lifting as the best, fastest, and most successful method of muscle-building yet discovered. It is a proven method, and the best way to prove it for yourself is to try it. Anybody who lifts weights progressively and regularly every other day for just three or four months will see tremendous gains in muscular growth and strength.

Today, weight-training is used by a great many athletes. Not only boxers and wrestlers, but also basketball, baseball and football players, and even track men, swimmers and judo experts, know they can improve their performance by training with weights. *All* athletes can.

Bob Kiphuth, the famous Yale swimming coach, knew the secret, too. Are you familiar with the incredible statistics? Over a 41-year period, the crack Yale team swam in 508 meets—and lost only four. Kiphuth trained his men on dry land for two solid months at the beginning of each season. They didn't swim. The only time they got under water was in the shower room. What kind of training did they get? Weight-training, and exercises: a routine muscle-building course.

We'll get into weight-lifting exercises in the next chapter. First, let's clear the air. There are a lot of people who still believe the old superstition that lightning never strikes twice in the same place, and there are also a lot of people who still believe the old superstitions about weight-lifting.

Are weight-lifters sluggish, muscular dolts who can barely bend their arms? Can weight-lifting make you musclebound? Is it "unnatural"? Will it hinder your flexibility? Today we know that all these questions can be answered simply: No.

As for flexibility, remember this: judo is a sport that requires a great deal of flexibility, and *judo champions train with weights*. So do gymnasts and acrobats, the most graceful and flexible of athletes.

You will not lose any flexibility or speed by developing your muscles. On the contrary, you'll gain in both areas. When coaches and athletes realized this, they began to use weight-training to great advantage. Today almost everybody uses it.

So don't let anybody kid you about the so-called dangers of weight-training. The ones who talk about getting musclebound are either envious or misinformed. There's no longer any question about it. Sports College, the independent research organization, says that training with weights can increase your proficiency in *any* sport, and that fears of becoming musclebound are unnecessary.

The athlete who uses weights is faster, stronger, lighter on his feet, and far more graceful and flexible than the average athlete who doesn't use weights. His endurance is better, and his heart and lungs and internal organs are stronger and healthier.

So much for superstitions. Now the question is: how do your muscles grow?

Muscles are made up of tiny muscle fibres—about four billion of them in your body. The average muscle fibre is about $1\frac{1}{4}$ inches in length, and 1/600 of an inch in diameter. If all your muscle fibres could be stretched out into one long thread, it could circle the globe four times!

What does exercise do to these fibres? It doesn't increase the *number* of fibres, but rather the size of the individual fibres. As you exercise, the parts of the fibre that have never worked before begin to work. Connective tissue becomes thicker and tougher. The tiny blood capillaries that feed the fibres increase in number. It's important that you know this, because these little capillaries are an essential factor in muscle growth. They bring oxygen and glycogen to the muscle fibres, and they carry waste material—mostly lactic acid—away from the fibres. You should lift weights every other day, rather than every day; the resting days provide time for the capillaries to grow. If you didn't give them time, you'd get a heavy accumulation of lactic acid in your body, and this brings on fatigue. So take the cue from your body, and give yourself plenty of rest.

Should you lift weights? By all means. Remember to do some warm-up exercises first, and also remember that weight-lifting is probably the most strenuous form of exercise known. I am assuming, of course, that there is nothing seriously wrong with your health to begin with. If you have had any kind of heart trouble, you should not attempt to lift weights unless you have first received permission from your doctor. There are many handicapped people who can benefit greatly from supervised weight-training.

Make sure you're in good health. Get a physical checkup before you begin, and tell your doctor you plan to start a weight-lifting program. When you have his consent—go to it!

6. Weight-Lifting

To most body-builders, weight-lifting is a very stimulating and enjoyable activity. To others, it is simply hard work—but well worth it. One thing is certain: there are no short-cuts. Once you decide to build your body by lifting weights, you must stick to it if you expect to see results. It isn't a system that works for some, and not for others. If you do stick to it, you *will* get results—and very satisfying ones. Weight-lifting will work for anyone who stays with it for just a few months.

Here are some terms you should know:

A *repetition* is one complete motion of a single exercise.

A specified number of repetitions—12, for instance, in the bench press—makes up a single *set*.

Definition refers to the sharpness of the muscle outline.

How to Exercise

Your weight-lifting session should never become a furious, breathtaking activity. It is important to rest between sets. If you are of average build, rest from three to five minutes between sets.

If you are underweight and want to gain, do fewer repetitions with slightly heavier weights, and take four- to five-minute rests between sets.

If you are overweight, or have considerable muscle bulk and

53

want greater definition, do more repetitions with somewhat lighter weights, and take shorter rests between sets. One to two minutes is sufficient.

Breathe regularly while exercising, as often and as deeply as you need. Never try to hold your breath. It is especially good to breathe deeply when doing the bench press.

It is not necessary to put an extra strain or tension on your muscles when exercising. The act of lifting the weight for the proper number of repetitions, and in correct form, will automatically tense the proper muscles.

When to Exercise

The amount of time you spend, and the regularity of your training, are both very important factors.

Don't make the mistake of trying to plunge in by lifting every day. No weight-lifter does. You should have three or four training periods a week, on alternate days. Each period should last from one to two hours. (Not all of this time should be devoted to weight-lifting activity. You should spend about twenty minutes or a half-hour in warming up with the exercises described in Chapter 4.)

Thus, you will be lifting weights one day, and resting the next. The resting days are just as important as the training days. Your muscles will grow, and your body will rest and rebuild itself, on the days off.

People who keep in shape with light calisthenics, or setting-up exercises, often like to do them in the morning, as soon as they awaken. The best time for weight-lifting, however, is at the other end of the day—in the evening, preferably just before going to bed. The reason for this will be clear after your first few sessions: weight-lifting is hard work. You will want to rest after lifting, and you won't want to tire yourself out at the beginning of the day.

As with swimming, you should wait at least a half hour after eating before exercising. If you are lifting weights in the late afternoon, plan your training session so that it ends about a half hour before your evening meal.

Food and Weight Control

One of the most attractive features of weight-lifting is that it tends to balance out your body. If you are overweight, it will help you reduce, and replace excess fat with muscle. If you are thin and underweight, it will build you up.

Nevertheless, all body-builders agree that diet is still the most important factor in controlling body weight. If you are underweight, your diet should include plenty of good, wholesome food: meat, butter, eggs, fresh fruits and vegetables, and plenty of milk and water every day. You can afford to eat the richer, fattier foods to help you put on a little weight: spaghetti and meatballs, mashed potatoes, and so on. But avoid heavily-seasoned foods.

And of course you should get plenty of rest. If you are under 21, you should be getting at least eight hours of sleep, and nine or ten is better.

If you are overweight, there is no substitute for cutting down on the *amount* of food you eat. Make sure that your diet is wholesome, rather than sweet or starchy. Keep away from fatty foods; eat baked potatoes without butter instead of mashed, and try to add more fish, chicken, calves' liver, and fresh fruits and vegetables to your meals.

The Basic Six

There are hundreds of different kinds of exercises you can do with weights, but most of them are far too specialized for the beginner. When you're starting out, you should concentrate on the exercises contained in these two chapters on weight-lifting. This chapter includes what many experts consider the Basic Six exercises: the bench press, regular press, squats, rowing motion, curls, and dead lift.

A great many of the specialized exercises are simply variations of these, designed to build up smaller muscle-groups for better definition.

As we take a closer look at the Basic Six, you'll see that each of them is an important exercise with a definite job to do. If you were to do nothing more than these six exercises, every other day for three months, you'd be astounded at your muscular improvement.

That doesn't mean, of course, that you *should* do "nothing more than these six exercises" for the next three months. A number of other important exercises are described in the following chapter, and the best program is to do half the total exercises on alternate training days.

For example, let's say that you've decided to exercise on Mondays, Wednesdays, and Fridays, and rest on Tuesdays, Thursdays, and weekends. On the first Monday, you would do two sets of the Basic Six. That means that you would go through the six exercises with the proper number of repetitions for each one, and then start at the beginning and go through the cycle of six exercises again.

On Tuesday you rest. On Wednesday you would do two sets of the exercises in the next chapter, and on the following Monday you would be back on the Basic Six.

Some people prefer to exercise every other day, including weekends, rather than three days a week, especially when they are starting out. This is perfectly all right; three days of rest per week is sufficient. But of course they should be *alternate* days. It would be very poor training to work out for four straight days, and rest for three.

The important thing is to choose a training schedule that you find convenient, and stick to it. *Regular* training with weights is the real "secret" of successful body-building. Occasional bursts of heavy training will do little if any good, and may be positively harmful.

In explaining the exercises, I have generally used the anatomical names for all muscles. You can learn them quickly by referring to the illustrated charts of body muscles in this chapter. Since these terms are actually used by body-builders and weight-lifters, and by many coaches and athletes, you will want to become familiar with them.

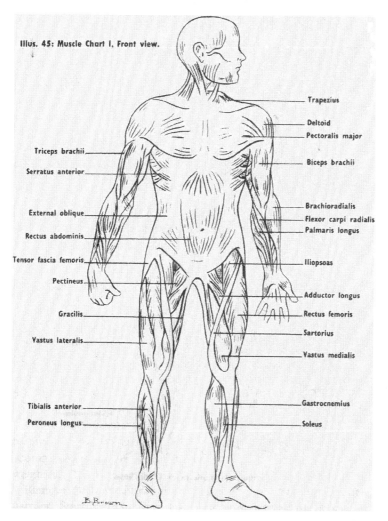

Illus. 45: Muscle Chart I, Front view.

Trapezius

Deltoid

Pectoralis major

Triceps brachii

Serratus anterior

Biceps brachii

Brachioradialis

External oblique

Flexor carpi radialis

Palmaris longus

Rectus abdominis

Tensor fascia femoris

Iliopsoas

Pectineus

Adductor longus

Gracilis

Rectus femoris

Sartorius

Vastus lateralis

Vastus medialis

Tibialis anterior

Gastrocnemius

Peroneus longus

Soleus

B.Brown

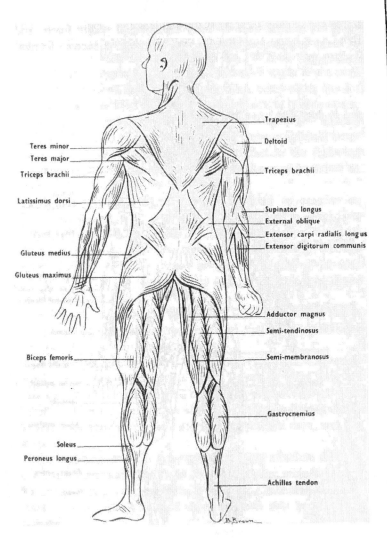

Teres minor
Teres major
Triceps brachii
Latissimus dorsi
Gluteus medius
Gluteus maximus
Biceps femoris
Soleus
Peroneus longus

Trapezius
Deltoid
Triceps brachii
Supinator longus
External oblique
Extensor carpi radialis longus
Extensor digitorum communis
Adductor magnus
Semi-tendinosus
Semi-membranosus
Gastrocnemius
Achilles tendon

Illus. 46: Muscle Chart II. Back view.

1. The *bench press* is the best single exercise for fast chest development. Specifically, it builds up the pectoral muscles, frontal deltoids, and triceps.

2. The *regular press* develops the arms (triceps) and shoulders.

3. *Squats* are the best-known leg developers—a popular exercise in paratrooper training units. Squats are excellent for building up the thighs, lungs and rib cage.

4. The *rowing motion* builds a strong back by developing the latissimus dorsi muscles, trapezius, and rear deltoids.

5. *Curls* are the famous biceps-builders, essential for strong arms.

6. The rowing motion develops the upper and middle parts of the back and sides; *dead lifts* take care of the all-important lower back muscle, or spinal erector.

How to Do the Basic Six

1. BENCH PRESS. Sometimes also called the back press, this requires the use of a low, sturdy bench and two bar supports. The bar supports are used to support the barbells while you take up your position on the bench. (If you're working with a partner, the bar supports are not absolutely necessary. He can hand the barbell to you when you're comfortably situated on the bench.)

Adjust the equipment so that you can first sit on the end of the bench with your knees bent comfortably, feet touching the floor. Then lie back on the bench so that your shoulders are under the barbell. Now you are in position to bring your hands back to your shoulders and grasp the barbell.

(Work with a light weight for the first two weeks: 30 or 40 pounds will be sufficient. Gradually work up to 50 pounds by adding 10 pounds per week; thereafter, continue to increase the weight slowly as you develop.)

Remove the barbell from the bar supports, or take it from your partner. Starting from chest level, push the barbell up to arms'

(Above) Illus. 47: The bench press. Your partner hands you the barbell if you do not have bar supports. (Below) Illus. 48: He stands by while you do the exercise.

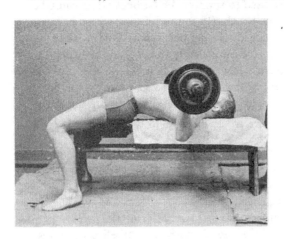

length, and return to chest level. Breathe deeply as you push upwards. Do 12 repetitions.

2. REGULAR PRESS. One of the three official Olympic lifts, this is also called the Two-Hands Military Press. In this press,

Illus. 50.

the weight is lifted with both hands straight from the floor to shoulder level in one continuous movement; then, after a two-second pause, the weight is pushed straight up to arms' length overhead. It is this latter movement that is properly called a press.

(Above) Illus. 51: The regular press, starting position.

(Below) Illus. 52: Press to arms' length.

The regular press is executed by pushing the barbell up from shoulder level, and returning it to shoulder level. The movement should be smooth and clean. Try to avoid jerky, uneven motions.

All the work is done by the arms and shoulders. The head and body are kept in a vertical position, and the legs are straight and stationary. It is important to avoid the natural tendency to arch the back. Do 12 repetitions, using a 30- or 40-pound weight.

3. SQUATS. In calisthenics, these are called Deep Knee Bends. In weight-lifting, and in the various Armed Forces, they're usually known as squats. A wonderful exercise, squats will develop powerful legs, and an enormous chest and lung capacity.

Illus. 53.

But quantity is as important here as quality: you must work up to a good number of repetitions, and they must be done right.

Place the bar of the barbell against the back of your neck and squat down, making sure to keep your head up and your back perfectly straight; then return to standing position. Use 40 or 50 pounds of weight.

Illus. 54: The squat with barbell. Work with a partner.

Try 12 repetitions for the first two weeks, then increase slowly to 15 or 20.

After the first month, when your legs have begun to build up, do as many *free squats* daily as you can. The free squat is a regular calisthenic, performed without using any weight at all, but with hands placed on hips.

Free squats are used to build powerful legs in paratrooper

training units. Even in Army basic training, a soldier must be able to do 75 free squats in order to achieve a grade of 100% in this exercise during the physical training tests. This is not to say, unfortunately, that every soldier can do it; but every body-builder should eventually work up to 100 squats.

A former body-builder in California recently decided to become a professional wrestler, and was dissatisfied with the size and strength of his legs. He put himself on a rigorous schedule of squats (free-style), and finally worked up to 1000 a day, in sets of 200 each. His chest and lungs benefited tremendously, of course, as well as his thighs, which finally measured 26 inches around. It can be done; but remember that he was a body-builder in fine shape to begin with.

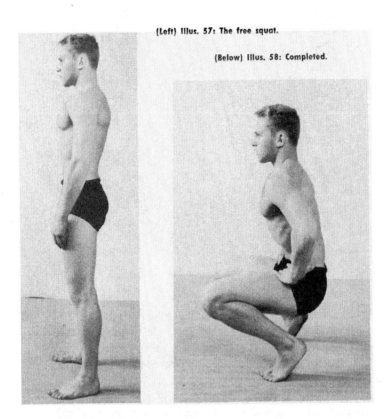

When you first begin, you'll find your thighs beginning to feel it after 20 or 25 free squats. Of course you should never push yourself to the point of exhaustion; take it easy in the beginning. After the first week or two, you won't have to worry about "straining" your thighs. They're the biggest, strongest muscles in your body, and they can take it.

4. ROWING MOTION. If you're looking for that V-shaped upper body, this is the exercise for you. The rowing motion develops not only the rear deltoids and the strong *trapezius* muscle in the center of the upper back, but also the *latissimus dorsi* or "wing" muscles—the ones that flare up from the sides of the rib cage right to the shoulders.

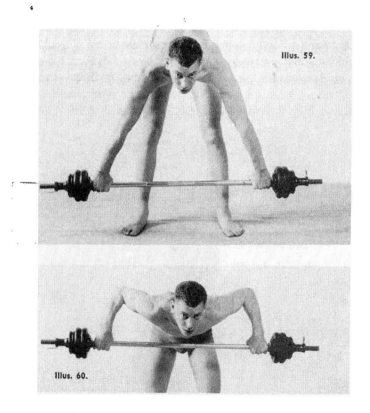

Illus. 59.

Illus. 60.

Bend at the waist so that upper body is parallel to the ground. Keep your legs and back straight. Pull the weight straight up to the neck, using your arms and shoulders to do all the work. Elbows are kept out wide, away from the body. Then lower barbell to straight-arm position. Do 12 repetitions, using 30 or 40 pounds to start.

5. CURLS. Whatever else you may be looking for, it's a sure bet you're in the market for a strong and powerful pair of arms. The biceps are the universal symbol of masculine strength. Trainees in most of the Armed Forces are required to do eight or ten pull-ups on the chinning bar before every meal. Yet, when they start basic training, many men can't get beyond the first two or three—and some can't chin themselves once. A great many boys neglect their arms because they seldom have to use them in civilian life. It's

Illus. 61: The curl with barbell.

a vicious circle: the boy who feels that his arms are weak may be afraid to play baseball and football—the very sports that could develop his arms.

You need solid arm power for throwing, lifting, pushing, pulling, climbing, hanging, carrying—and, in an emergency, for self-defense fighting. The weight-lifter's curl is the best and fastest way to develop the all-important biceps muscle.

A regular overhand grip was used in all the previous exercises. In the normal curl, an underhand grip is used to develop the biceps. An overhand grip is used (reverse curl) to build up the forearm muscles as well as the biceps.

Either a barbell or dumbbells may be used. Start with 15 or

Illus. 62: The curl, regular underhand grip.

20 pounds, and work up to 30 or more. Stand erect, holding weight at arms' length. Bring the weight in a semi-circular path up to shoulder level, keeping elbows at sides. The back is kept straight; don't allow yourself to bend backwards or move your elbows back. Do 12 repetitions.

Illus. 63: The curl, reverse (overhand) grip.

6. DEAD-LIFT. Two grips are possible: a regular overhand grip, or a combination grip—one hand over, one under. Use whichever you prefer. Some body-builders like to use the combination grip when the barbell is straddled.

In the starting position, the weight is on the floor. It may either be straddled, or approached from one side. Grasp the bar, keeping arms straight, and simply straighten the legs and body. Lifting is done with the lower back muscles, not with the arms or shoulders. Do 10 repetitions.

In the beginning, use a light weight—not more than 60 pounds. Slowly work up to 75 and 100.

A note of caution here: No matter how powerful your arms and shoulders may be, never try to lift a heavy weight from the ground unless you've been doing dead-lifts in your weight-training program. The lower back muscle, or spinal erector, is an important

(Above) Illus. 64: The dead lift, straddle position.

(Below) Illus. 65: Note the combination grip.

71

Illus. 66: The dead lift, approach from the side.

foundation muscle, enabling you to walk upright. With regular attention and development, it will become a powerful muscle, capable of supporting tremendous amounts of weight. It can be strained, however, if you attempt a heavy dead-lift without previous training.

Therefore, start your program with a weight you can handle easily, and you'll never have any trouble. The rule for safety is this: In the dead-lift, never use a weight that you cannot lift without straining for at least five repetitions.

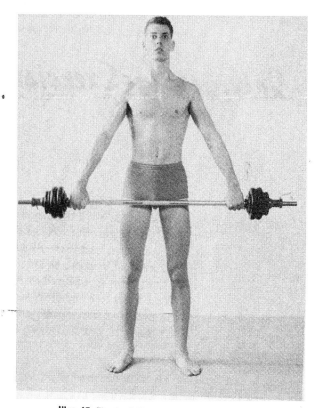

Illus. 67: The dead lift, regular overhand grip.

7. Interesting Exercises

The Basic Six exercises are designed to build the major muscle groups—arms, back, chest, trunk and thighs. But you can also use your imagination to make up your own exercises. Almost any exercise you do, no matter how unusual, is good, as long as you don't overdo it. Here are six to start with—specialized exercises to build your calf muscles, which are likely to be ignored, and other muscle groups you'll want to develop. After you've worked on these, think up your own variations if you find your training program getting monotonous.

Calf-Builder

A fairly common mistake of beginners is to concentrate on building just the upper body. Even if you include squats, poor calf development can spoil the effect of an otherwise excellent physique. Here's how to look good from the knees down.

Standing erect, feet apart, support the barbell across the shoulders against the back of your neck. With your hands grasp the bar near the inside collars.

Keeping your back and legs straight, slowly raise up as high as possible on your toes; then return to standing position.

Start with 24 repetitions. You'll get the best results if you do

12 times with your toes pointed out and the next 12 with toes pointed in. This is the surest way to develop both parts of the two-headed calf muscle, or *gastrocnemius*.

Illus. 68: The calf-builder.

Some body-builders stand with the balls of their feet on a plank or 2×4, so that heels can be lowered down to the floor, thus stretching and building calf muscles even more. This is not essential, and some physical education specialists do not recommend it, while others do. In any case, you shouldn't worry about it until you're ready for advanced development; then it's up to you.

Start with a 30- or 40-pound barbell for this exercise and work up to about half your body weight. If you weigh less than 100 pounds, start with a 20-pound weight and work up.

Pull-Over

This is good for developing the flaring *latissimus dorsi* muscles of the back, and the *pectoralis major* (chest muscles).

Lie on your back with your knees drawn up to your chest, legs crossed at the ankles, feet not touching the floor. Extend your arms beyond the head, elbows locked so that arms are straight. Use light dumbbells, 10 pounds each, or just the bar of a barbell with no weights added.

Illus. 69: The pull-over. You may prefer to keep both legs on the mat.

To do one repetition, raise the weight in a short 90-degree arc to a position directly above the chest, keeping arms and back straight; then return to starting position. It is important to do the work with your chest and side muscles, and without arching your back. Do 10 repetitions.

Press Behind Neck

This is like the regular press, except that you start with the barbell resting on your shoulders against the back of your neck—

Illus. 70: The press behind the neck.

the same starting position used for the calf-builder. Press the bar up to arms' length overhead, then lower it to starting position. Keep the knees and back straight.

Illus. 71: Completed.

This press, in addition to building the triceps and shoulders, will also develop the important *trapezius* muscle of the upper back; and it's an excellent exercise if you're round-shouldered. So is the pull-over, above. Do 12 repetitions.

Side-Bend

Muscles often ignored or neglected by beginners are those at the sides of the waist, called the external and internal oblique muscles. They shouldn't be forgotten; side-bending is important in developing a strong trunk.

You can do the exercise with a dumbbell or barbell. Since both methods are good, you can use them in alternate training sessions.

Illus. 72: The side-bend.

1. Place the bar across your shoulders, behind your neck, as in the preceding exercise. Use just the bar; side-bends should be done with the same amount of weight you use in the curl. Bend to one side as far as possible, then to the other side, and return to the starting position. That's one repetition. Don't bend your knees or allow yourself to bend forward. All the work should be done at the waist. Start with 10 repetitions and slowly work up to 20, adding weight when you feel you can use it.

2. Use a single dumbbell. Stand erect, arms at sides, holding the dumbbell in your right hand. Bend to the right side, then to the left, and back to the starting position. Again, that counts as one repetition. Do 10 times with the dumbbell in your right hand, then 10 with the weight in your left.

Shoulder Shrug

This is a specialized exercise to develop the diamond-shaped *trapezius* muscle, which slopes down from the back of the neck out to the deltoids, and then down to converge at the center of the back.

Illus. 73: The shoulder shrug.

Stand erect, feet apart, holding the barbell at arms' length across your thighs. Grasp the bar near the inside collars.

The action is simple. Lift your shoulders upward as far as possible in a slow shrug, keeping the arms straight.

Start with a 30- or 40-pound barbell and gradually work up to about half your body weight. At first, do 12 repetitions.

79

Alternate Press

Extra work on curls can produce good biceps, but it's the triceps that give your upper arms a full, rounded effect and add a great deal of strength. This alternate press, done with dumbbells, develops the triceps and deltoids.

Stand erect, feet apart, holding dumbbells at shoulder level. (Use a weight you can handle, between 10 and 25 pounds. Add weight later, as you develop.)

Illus. 74: The alternate press.

Illus. 75: The alternating
movement.

Lift the weight in your right hand to arm's length overhead, then lower to shoulder level. As the right arm is lowered, push the dumbbell in the left hand up to arm's length. Continue this alternate movement for 10 repetitions. One repetition is completed when you have done a press with both arms.

When you want variety or special emphasis on a particular muscle group, you can find many other exercises in books and magazines devoted to weight training. And remember: There's nothing wrong with making up your own variations.

8. Self-Defense

The rest of this book deals with self-defense. You should understand that there are a number of self-defense techniques, all of them very effective. Many people in this country have heard about *karate* by now, but there are still plenty who think that all methods of unarmed defense are called *judo*. Judo is a highly specialized sport, with a definite etiquette, forms and throws. Kicking, for example, is not a part of judo; striking out with the hands is not judo. Judo today is practiced as a sport, although it was developed as a method of self-defense.

In addition to judo and karate, there is *savate*, the French method of foot-defense; *jiu-jitsu*, includes judo but has additional throws, chops, and special defenses; *aikido* is the art of twisting and bending the joints, and taking advantage of your opponent's maneuvers; *yawara* is used in conjunction with aikido to provide effective wrist-holds, arm-locks, body-holds, and chokes, and the defenses against all of these.

The list is far from exhausted. There is the excellent and scientific Chinese method of *cheena-adi*, a kind of judo-jiu-jitsu combination; the Indian art of *lathie*, or stick defense; the Japanese *kempo*, a "hard" art of self-defense against armed opponents; and even the Irish *shillelagh*, or cudgel-play. There is

American Marine fighting, a combination of jiu-jitsu, boxing, wrestling, brawling, and a few other techniques thrown in. The Indian *Gusthi*, or wrestling, is also a form of sporting combat.

So remember that judo is but a single art, an excellent one, but hardly the last word on self-defense. The methods described in the following chapters are actually called *ketsugo*—the Japanese word for combination. These methods represent the best and most basic techniques, selected from a number of the different forms of self-defense mentioned above. Only the throws can really be called judo.

What about the men who have mastered these skills—what are they like? It's interesting that they have a characteristic philosophy and disposition. They're almost always of a gentle, pleasant, and peaceable nature. Why? Well—why not? They can afford to be. They wouldn't think of starting or provoking a fight, because they have no need to prove themselves. They've demonstrated their powers many times. Instead of chips on their shoulders, they have quiet, firm confidence in their own abilities.

They learn these techniques, not in order to be aggressive fighters or troublemakers, but simply to be able to protect and defend themselves and their families.

Most of these methods, in fact, were developed hundreds of years ago in Asia and the Orient, often by peasants and monks who had no weapons. This was the only way they could defend themselves against the numerous bandits and robbers who roamed the countryside at night.

Throughout the world, those who have learned these methods have always retained the ancient philosophy of self-defense: Never provoke or encourage a fight. Fight only to protect and defend yourself, or someone who is being bullied. Maintain a high regard for gentlemanly conduct and good sportsmanship. Some of the world's top-ranking judo experts have been praised by their fellows for refusing to demonstrate their powers when provoked by mere words. They will defend themselves, of course, if attacked, but they will never "demonstrate" just to show off. (Official judo demonstrations, tournaments, and exhibitions are not in the "show-off" category.)

I have never met or heard of a self-defense expert who was not a person of honor and courtesy.

As you increase your skill in self-defense, you'll find that you're automatically better at keeping your wits about you in a dangerous situation. You won't scare as easily. This is one of the wonderful benefits of self-defense training.

A few years ago, a small group of people were sitting in a café in New York City. There were two young ladies in the group, and one of them happened to be unusually pretty. There was also a judo expert in the party—a mild, pleasant man in his fifties.

These people were annoyed by a group of wise-talking hoodlums who made remarks about the girl. One of them finally came up and put his hand on her shoulder. He had no sooner touched her than he was thrown back violently against the wall by the old judo expert—*who never left his chair!*

The rest of the gang came at him, and went flying. The judo expert remained seated; he was merely moving his arms, with apparently little effort. In fact, he continued talking to the group all this time!

Yes, it sounds incredible. But it's quite true. The man, of course, was a judo master, with a lifetime of practice and training behind him. There wasn't much he didn't know about balance and self-defense. And any judo expert will tell you that it's quite possible to throw somebody while you're sitting in a chair, if you know your judo.

How Important Is Strength?

Judo is often referred to as "the *gentle* art of self-defense." While it is true that no great strength is needed to master most of these self-defense techniques, it would be foolish to think that strength is not important. In man-to-man combat, strength is always important. It may not be the decisive factor, but only an expert in self-defense can afford to disregard it.

If we were to set up a contest between two students who had identical skill in judo, but were of unequal strength, the stronger would win every time. It's a mistake to think that you can rely solely on self-defense tricks and fast maneuvers. Speed and clever strategy are good; indeed, they are essential. But they may not be.enough. They can be used to best advantage only when the body is strong and flexible. While regular self-defense training will itself help to toughen the body, it should be supplemented by a vigorous program of body-building and weight-training. This is the kind of program used by the world judo champions.

How to Practice

Every self-defense technique involves a certain logical sequence of steps. They must be described that way, and you will find it easiest to practice that way—first you do this, then that, and now this. What you should aim for, though, is not a series of individual movements, but one smooth, speedy, continuous motion.

When you practice with a partner, go through the motions slowly, even stopping if necessary to refer to the pictures and text again. Make sure your balance, body position, and stance are right at each point. Continue in this manner, slow-motion, until you are able to blend the movements together slowly. Then increase your speed. Repeat the entire technique a few times to make sure you have learned it; now let your partner practice.

These techniques have been described from the point of view of the right-handed person. Once you have gained proficiency from this side, of course, you should reverse the directions and practice them from the left side as well. No matter how long you train in judo, you can't begin to call yourself an expert until you can perform any maneuver from either side.

What to Wear

Assuming that you do not have a regular judo outfit, remember to wear old and sturdy clothes when practicing. Dungarees are

Illus. 76: The Judo costume.

excellent. The shirt is sometimes a problem: ideally, it should be heavy enough to resist being torn. Otherwise, it should be old enough so that it won't matter if it is torn. A sturdy work-shirt will usually do the trick.

Where to Practice

The use of a mat is recommended wherever possible. However, lack of a mat should not prevent you from practicing most of these self-defense techniques. A soft, grassy area, free of stones and other debris, will serve just as well. Putting down a couple of blankets is good, too. The shoulder and somersault throws are the only ones that require a padded mat.

Balance

In all self-defense, balance is the essential element. The object, of course, is to maintain your own balance while breaking or disturbing your opponent's.

Your balance will be "weak to the front"—meaning you have poor balance, and can be pulled or pushed forward easily—when your weight is on the toes of both feet. It is "weak to the back" when your weight is on both heels; you can be pushed or pulled backwards easily.

The weakest position of all is that in which you balance on one foot. Here you may be pushed easily in any direction.

In the *strongest* fighting position, the feet are perpendicular (at right angles) to one another, and the body is twisted slightly, as in Illustration 77.

Practice your balance. Again I emphasize that this is the most important part of self-defense. Some beginners fail to realize this, because they have come to judo after hearing "you don't have to be strong."

It is the gentle art—but why? Why is it called the *soft* art, the *yielding* art? Because that's just what you do. You yield—up to a point. You act weak, as though you're a pushover.

Let's say an antagonist is pushing you around. He puts his big fat paws on your chest and pushes. What do *you* do?

You let him push. Try to stand firm, as though you're simply resisting him; but don't step forward, and don't push back.

Illus. 77: The fighting stance. A strong balance position.

When he feels resistance, the bully pushes harder. Now you might take half a step back, or two or three small steps if he's really much stronger.

Who has the advantage of balance at this point? You do, of course. You're standing still, or taking very short steps backward. You can easily maintain your center of balance.

But your opponent is pushing forward, and leaning forward.

So instead of pushing back, you quickly grab his wrists or coat-sleeves, and *pull him forward*—hard. Chances are Bully Doakes will fall flat on his face, as he pitches past you.

That, very simply, is what we mean when we talk about taking advantage of your opponent's balance. All judo throws, and many other self-defense techniques, are designed to catch the other guy off balance, or *put* him off balance, and give you the upper hand.

The Starting Position

When working on the throws with a partner, always assume the standard judo starting position. Facing partner, grasp the underside of his right sleeve, just below the elbow, with your left hand, and his left lapel with your right hand. Your partner takes the same grip on you.

Illus. 78: The starting position and grip.

In a self-defense situation, you would try to grip your opponent in roughly the same way, whenever possible.

How to Move

Once you have the grip, you and your partner begin to move and maneuver about the mat. The way you move is important. Don't pick your feet up too high; you're more likely to lose your balance that way. The best technique is a kind of gliding movement, in which the feet slide lightly over the mat, sometimes touching it, and seldom lifted more than an inch. Try not to cross one foot in front or in back of the other—that also weakens your balance.

9. How to Fall

If you don't want to get hurt, learn how to fall. If you want to build up your confidence for self-defense training, learn how to fall. If you ever expect to go on to advanced judo, learn how to fall.

In short, you *must* learn how to fall. This is the most important part of your preparation. Don't make the mistake that most beginners do: They ignore the falls because the falls don't seem important or because they think they already know how to fall.

If you were to sit in on any judo class, you'd see that the students spend the first lesson or two just on falls. After that, they devote at least ten minutes of each session practicing and warming up on falls; and this includes the most advanced students and judo masters.

Why is it so important? Simply because you can't practice this kind of self-defense unless you do know how to fall. It's too dangerous. You can get hurt badly without a good falling technique; but *with* a good technique, there's little or no chance that you'll hurt yourself at all.

Where will you be when you really need your self-defense training? You won't be on a mat. You may not be on grass. You may very well be in the city, or on a hard concrete or asphalt surface, and possibly walking along with a date.

If you get knocked down, knowing how to fall will keep you

from getting hurt, and it will help you to bounce back up. Once you learn how to fall, hard surfaces won't be as dangerous. After a month or two of practice, you'll automatically fall the right way. There's nothing magical about falling; you can still get scratched or bruised on a hard surface, but that's a lot better than breaking a bone or hitting your head. The best way to warm up for any self-defense practice is to work on your falls.

The most important thing is to roll with the fall, which means that your body goes into a natural curl as soon as you start to fall. It does not mean that you just crumple up, or relax like a soggy dishrag. In the curl, your chin is tucked down onto your chest, and your knees are pulled up toward your chest.

Illus. 79: The natural falling curl.

Never try to break your fall with stiff arms, or with your hands out. Your aim in falling is to develop an easy, controlled roll. The body should not be tense; you can maintain the curl without being stiff.

While you don't break your fall with stiff arms or hands out, you do use your arms to break the fall, in this way: just as you hit the mat or ground, slap down hard with your arm. (Whether you

92

use both arms or just one will depend on the kind of fall you're taking.)

Using your arm (or arms) to break the fall this way accomplishes three things: it gives you a natural shock-absorber, helps you bring the roll to a stop, and prepares you for a quick recovery and rebound to your feet.

To understand the arm motion clearly, lie on your back on the mat, with your head forward and chin tucked into your chest and your knees drawn up toward your head. Keep your arms extended flat, palms down, for support. This is the actual position in which you land in the backward fall. Now raise your arms up well in the air, and bring them down hard on the mat, letting them bounce up naturally. This is what actually breaks your fall.

Your whole arm, from shoulder to fingertips, should strike the mat at the same time. If you keep your arms relaxed during this

93

motion, you'll find that you won't get hurt. But this does not mean that you should hit the mat lightly. On the contrary, don't be afraid to hit it hard. "Relaxed" means that your arms should not be stiff, and the muscles should not be tense.

Your arms should always be in front of you when you're falling, and should hit the mat first.

Let's consider the four basic falls in more detail. Practice them in order, since they range from the easiest and most common (falls to the side) to the most unusual and difficult (forward fall from stand). The falls to the side and back are by far the most useful, and should be mastered thoroughly before you go on to the others.

Falls to the Side

ROLLS TO RIGHT AND LEFT. Assume the same position as before, lying on your back with your body curled, head forward (chin tucked in), and knees drawn up toward chest. Instead of bringing

Illus. 81: The rolling fall to the right.

both arms up, however, this time roll to your right, and strike the mat with your right arm to break the "fall." Your left arm should be folded across your chest in a comfortable position.

Practice the same roll to the left, beating the mat with your left arm.

ALTERNATE ROLL TO BOTH SIDES. Now combine the two, so that you're rolling in a continuous movement from one side to the other, striking the mat with the proper arm each time. This is an excellent warm-up, since it will introduce you to the roll and help you get acquainted with the feeling of movement in a good curl position.

There is no special number of "times" to do this exercise; there is a natural tendency, as in weight-lifting, to concentrate on the count rather than on the proper form. It's easy to cheat yourself without meaning to. Therefore, do the alternate roll until you've had enough, but always concentrate on doing it *well*, which really means three things:

1. Keep your head forward always, chin tucked in.

95

2. Beat down hard with the proper arm. In the backward fall, use both arms.

3. Keep your arms and body-curl relaxed.

Now you can start to try some height, so that you're really falling. Begin your rolls from a squatting position, instead of lying on your back, and practice the falls to right and left. Start to swing your arm down as soon as you begin to fall; your arm should hit the mat a fraction of a second before your body does. This is what actually breaks the fall, and helps you to bounce back up again. Remember to keep your head tucked into your chest.

When you've mastered the falls to right and left sides from the squatting position, you're ready to get even more height by gradually straightening your knees at the start. Continue increasing your height from the mat until you can fall to either side from a standing position.

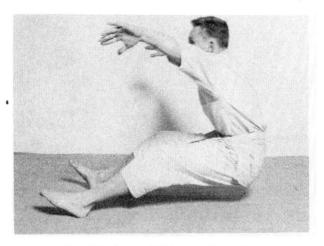

Backward Fall

If you've ever done any tumbling, you may already have mastered this fall. At any rate, you already know the position in which you land on the mat. The backward fall is essentially the same as the falls to the side, except that both arms are used simultaneously to beat down on the mat. Lie on your back on the mat, head and chin tucked into chest, knees drawn up, and arms extended flat on the mat for support. This is the position in which you land.

It will be an easy step to achieve the backward fall next from a sitting position, but not so easy to master it from a full stand. Take your time on this; gradually straighten your knees, getting a little more height with each session. You're doing well if you can perform a good, confident backward fall from a full standing position at the end of two or three weeks of steady practice.

Forward Somersault Fall

Also called the Forward Rolling Fall, this is not exactly the same as the forward somersault in tumbling and gymnastics. For one thing, the object of this fall is not necessarily to land back on your feet. Things move quickly on the judo mat, as they do in real self-defense situations. You can't count on your ability to convert every forward fall into a somersault. What you can usually do, however, is turn it into a break-fall. (All of the various falls are often and correctly called break-falls by judo experts.)

Further, you do not roll directly forward over your head and back in the forward somersault fall; the object is to cushion the fall with the right or left shoulder. Thus, you will be rolling diagonally forward to the right or left.

Assume a squatting position on the mat, resting on the balls of your feet rather than on your heels. Push yourself forward to let

98

your hands down to the mat, palms down. Your hands should be about 18 inches from your toes. You will automatically point yourself in the right direction for a left-shoulder forward fall if you place your left hand in front of your left foot, and your right hand between your feet. Tuck your chin into your chest.

All that remains is to push yourself off your toes, into a rolling diagonal somersault. If you are rolling first to the left, the back of your head should just barely touch the mat—or, even better, not

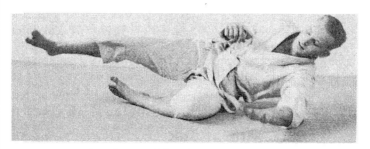

Illus. 87: The end of the forward somersault fall.

99

touch it at all—with the brunt of the fall being taken by the back of your left shoulder and back.

The forward somersault roll to the diagonal left will bring you across to the right side of your back. Thus, you beat down on the mat with your right arm and hand to break the fall. The situation is reversed, of course, if you take the forward roll to the diagonal right.

Illus. 88: The diagonal end of a forward fall.

When you have mastered this relatively easy forward roll to right and left sides from the squatting position, try it next from a low crouch, and finally from a high crouch. In this last stage, your right foot is placed somewhat forward (if you are rolling to the diagonal right) and your body is bent forward from the waist until both palms are touching the mat in the positions described earlier. Your knees are bent slightly. Your position will now roughly resemble a sprinter's starting crouch, except that your head is tucked in.

Illus. 89: The forward fall from a stand.

Forward Fall from Stand

This is the most difficult of all falls, and is seldom used in actual judo practice or competition. Nevertheless, it may be necessary in self-defense, and is always taught in advanced judo classes. It is also an excellent warm-up exercise. This forward fall is the only one in which you do not go into a curl or somersault.

To achieve it, fall forward from a standing position, bending your body only slightly and breaking the fall with your hands and forearms, as shown above. Your head, body, and knees are thus protected. Note that you do not bend at the knees or waist. Your body is kept straight.

Practice the fall first from a kneeling position. This will help you get accustomed to the idea of breaking your fall with forearms and palms; remember to beat down on the mat with both forearms and hands simultaneously.

Finally, practice the fall from a full standing position. As you tip forward slowly on your toes, the upper half of your body is bent forward in order to achieve a slight convex curve—convex in

Illus. 90: Landing position in the forward fall from stand.

relation to the final position of the body on the ground. (Again, see illustration above.)

Judo masters do not consider themselves expert in performing this fall until they can land successfully after throwing themselves into the air from a short running jump. It is a most impressive stunt in any judo exhibition, but requires a great deal of practice. No beginner should attempt it until he has mastered all the other falls.

10. Ketsugo, Judo and Jiu-Jitsu

Now that you know how to fall, you're ready for self-defense. In this chapter you'll learn some of the most basic and important throws and maneuvers: the shoulder throw, hip throw, side-sweep, somersault throw, arm-lock and throw, and the swinging arm-lock and twist throw. All of these are excellent and effective, and all are potentially dangerous. Use them only when you mean business.

What can you do when somebody stronger grabs you? The second part of this chapter takes up two useful methods of release: the release from three different kinds of wrist-holds, and the release from a choke-hold.

The throws are balance and leverage techniques, and require no great strength, but they take a lot of practice before you can begin to call yourself an expert. And remember: while strength is not *required*, it definitely gives you a great advantage. So you would be wise not to separate body-building and self-defense; they belong together.

103

PART I—THE THROWS

Shoulder Throw

What do you visualize when you think of judo? If you're like most people, you probably think of the dramatic over-shoulder throw, in which your opponent is thrown or "flipped" over your back. This is one of the most effective maneuvers in self-defense.

There's nothing mysterious or difficult about the throw, and it should be mastered because it's a good defense against a number of attacks. Let's go through it in slow motion.

Facing your partner, grasp his right elbow with your left hand, (see below). Step in close to his body, pivoting around so that you're facing the same direction he is. As you perform the turn, bring your right hand under his right arm, grasping his upper arm close to the shoulder (Illus. 92).

Illus. 91: Shoulder throw, starting position.

Illus 92: Second stage of the shoulder throw.

Now you have a good grip. Pull his right arm forward as you bend your upper body forward, and your partner will be pulled over your right shoulder and back, and down onto the mat (Illus. 93, 94, 95).

An excellent variation of this is to sink down low as you pivot in and around, keeping your knees bent. As you move into the throw, straighten your legs quickly. This alone will lift your partner off the mat, and the forward-bending motion will complete the throw.

Illus. 93: In mid-air in the shoulder throw.

Illus. 94: About to land.

Illus. 95: The landing.

This variation is good, and should be used, when both partners are about the same height. When the other person is considerably taller, use the bending-forward technique alone.

The shoulder throw, like every other move in self-defense, should be practiced until you can do it without thinking about the steps. In the first session, practice the throw slowly, step by step, until you have the idea. Do it that way two or three times. Then reverse positions, and let your partner practice. The one who is being thrown should have no trouble taking this fall on his shoulder and back.

After that, you should be able to perform the throw in a smooth, quick, continuous motion. *Speed is essential.* In a real self-defense situation, of course, nobody waits around for you to get the proper position or the right grip. You may never be able to duplicate exactly the maneuvers you learn in practice, so you should always be ready to improvise.

In the shoulder throw, for example, suppose you can't get a good grip on your opponent's elbow—what then? Simply try to get hold of his sleeve, forearm, or wrist. The general idea is to learn to recognize the basic and important motions in each technique, and practice them with your own variations.

The shoulder throw is extremely effective, and must therefore be practiced with care. There are three rules that should always be observed when you're working with a partner:

1. It goes without saying that both you and your partner should know how to fall. Before attempting the throw, always warm up with a few front falls and forward rolling falls.

2. Always practice this one on a mat.

3. Never let go of your partner. Repeat: *Never let go of your partner*. Hang on tight to his right arm, especially at the height of the throw, and continue to hang on until after he's landed on the mat. Remember that you'll both be practicing the throw, and you'll certainly want him to hang on, too. The one who is doing the throwing can help break his partner's fall by pulling up on his right arm or sleeve as he's about to hit the mat. The partner who is being thrown uses his left arm, shoulder and back to break the fall.

The Hip Throw

One of the most basic, most important, most useful, and most spectacular throws in judo is the hip throw. It is also one of the hardest to learn and master, because most beginners tend to make certain natural mistakes. Don't allow yourself to become discouraged. Get a patient partner or instructor, and practice this on a mat. *Anyone* can learn the throw; and once you've learned it, you can throw almost anyone, regardless of weight or strength.

Therefore, if you find that you are failing to execute the throw properly, never assume that your partner is too heavy, or that you lack sufficient strength. These are natural assumptions among beginners, and they are almost always wrong. Most failures are due to improper placement of feet, and failure to understand the correct action of the hip.

Illus. 96: The start of the hip throw.

Face your opponent, assuming standard posture and grip. Take a short step forward with your right foot, pointing your toes toward the inner side of your opponent's right foot. This means that your own body will turn to the left, beginning the pivot that you will quickly complete. Simultaneously, release your hold on your opponent's left lapel, and slide your right hand and arm around your opponent's waist. As you complete the pivot, you will have your back to opponent, and your body in close contact with his. Note carefully that you do *not* try to step to the outside of your opponent's feet. Correct pivoting action and stance will bring your feet within his. This is your first objective.

109

The actual throwing is done with the hip as the central pivot. This action, too, must be clearly understood.

First, your hips must be lower than opponent's hips. Unless your opponent is taller, therefore, this means that you must bend your knees. The action of straightening your knees and bending forward, pushing your hips *back* into him, and pulling down on his right sleeve with your left hand, will lift your opponent off the mat. Note that you do not try to lift your opponent *up* with your hips; you drive his hips *back*, and he will be lifted onto your own

Illus. 98: Completing the hip throw.

hips and across your back. Now you continue the pivot, twisting around to the left with your left hip, still pulling down with your left hand. Your opponent will be balanced on and then pulled over your right hip; when you turn further and move away from beneath him, he is unsupported and falls down on the mat.

It is not always necessary or essential to release your opponent's left lapel and slide the right hand around his waist. The standard grip may be retained throughout the throw, and this may increase the surprise value of your attack. However, it is more difficult to learn the throw this way, and you would do well to put your right hand around his waist until you have mastered the basic technique.

The Side-Sweep

One of the trickiest and most effective throws, the side-sweep is especially good against an opponent who has no knowledge of judo. It can also be used, of course, against another student, but he is much more likely to be expecting it. Against the uninitiated, the side-sweep comes like a bomb out of nowhere—he's being swept through the air before he knows what hit him.

In fact, he may never really know how he was thrown. This is one of the strange, valuable and bewildering effects of certain judo techniques. The gestures, especially in this throw, are smooth and almost gentle, rather than violent. Instead of pushing, you yield—momentarily. Your partner or opponent is continually pushing, and shifting his weight. Then, suddenly, as he is changing his center of balance, your yielding becomes a weapon. In one co-ordinated movement, you actually do three things: pull, push,

112

Illus. 100: Sweeping
opponent's right foot
to the left.

and sweep. Yet no strength is needed. It's the sudden loss of balance, not force, that does the trick.

A little practice is necessary to master the sense of timing and coordination of three simultaneous movements. But the practice is well worth it: the side-sweep seldom fails, and can be used very easily against a bigger and stronger opponent.

In this maneuver especially, you must keep your eyes on your opponent's feet. One who is unfamiliar with judo is likely to watch your face, thinking he can read your intentions. Actually, this makes him doubly vulnerable.

Assume standard position and grip: with your left hand grasp the underside of your opponent's right sleeve, and with your right hand grasp his upper left lapel. (During practice, of course, your partner will have the same grip on you.)

As you begin to maneuver and circle about the mat, you yield

momentarily to your partner's attempts to push you backwards, or to your left side. Wait until he is in the process of shifting his weight forward to his right foot. Your object is to sweep your opponent's right foot to his left side, just before his foot comes down again on the mat.

Contact is made with your opponent's outer right ankle. Turn your left foot—the sweeping foot—in to the side and up, so that the bottom of your foot is hitting your opponent's ankle.

As you perform the sweeping movement, you must simultaneously pull *down* on opponent's right sleeve, and *up* on his left lapel. The sweeping action alone is not always sufficient to throw your opponent, particularly if you have misjudged his balance and distribution of weight.

114

The side-sweep sounds complicated. Can you really use it on a bully? Absolutely. It's the ideal throw when you're grappling with him, or when he grabs you from the front.

Somersault Throw

In judo tournaments, this is considered a sacrifice throw, since you deliberately choose to risk a backward fall to the mat in order to execute the somersault throw, sometimes also called the overhead throw.

In self-defense, it is an excellent surprise throw against an opponent who attempts to grab or push you. First, try to obtain something close to the standard grip on opponent's right sleeve and left lapel; or grasp both arms, or both lapels. It is important that you have a good grip with both hands.

Illus. 103: Falling back for the somersault throw.

As your opponent pushes, you let yourself suddenly sink back and down to the ground, curling into a backward fall, and pulling your opponent forward. The closer you are to your opponent when you begin to fall, the more effectively you can execute this throw. It is difficult to perform at arms' length. Maintain a tight curl as you sit down; try to land just in back of your own left heel.

As you begin to pull your opponent over, bring your right foot up and under your opponent's stomach. The power of your right leg is then used to lift your opponent off the ground and to throw him over your head. The idea is not to *kick* your opponent in the stomach, but to use your foot for a lifting and pushing action.

Use your arms throughout to pull your opponent forward, over,

116

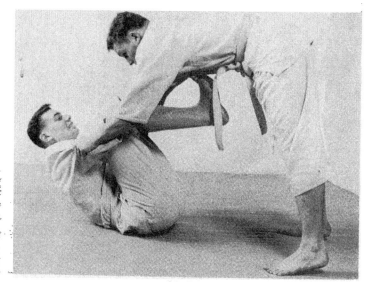

(Above) Illus. 104: Bringing the right foot up.

Illus. 105: Lifting opponent up.

117

Illus. 106: The somersault throw completed.

and down. Practice this one only on a mat, and only with a partner who can perform the forward rolling fall.

Finally, this is not a good technique to use if you are much shorter than your partner or opponent.

Arm-Lock and Throw

This is an excellent leverage technique, as popular among FBI and Army Intelligence agents as it is among youngsters learning the rudiments of self-defense. The great value of the arm-lock is that it provides a technique which may be used to restrain and control an opponent who may be annoying or harassing, but not really dangerous. The show-off or bully is put in his place nicely with this technique, which is more humiliating than painful.

118

Illus. 107: Grasping wrist for arm-lock.

It is not really a judo technique, although it is Oriental. It looks impressively like judo, however, and should in itself be enough to convince anyone that you've been trained in self-defense.

If your opponent's right hand is coming down from above, grasp his wrist with your own right hand so that your palm is turned outward, that is, toward your right side (see above).

If your opponent's hand is reaching for you, or pushing, at chest level, use a normal overhand grip when you grasp his wrist. In order to force his arm to bend upwards, use a chop: strike hard at the inside of his right elbow joint with the outer side of your left palm. (The chop is the kind of blow used in karate.)

Now bring your left hand up in back of your opponent's right arm, between his forearm and biceps, and under his arm to grasp your own right wrist (see page 120). Pulling down on your right

Illus. 108: Left hand comes into action in the arm-lock.

wrist with your left hand and bending forward will easily force your opponent backwards and down. You can now bring him to the ground if necessary. Simple arm pressure will take him down smoothly. Kicking his right leg out from under him with your own leg or thigh will do the job more forcefully.

This is also an excellent defense against a knife attack when the thrust comes from above. Use your right forearm to parry the downward thrust, and capture your opponent's wrist quickly. This takes speed. But speed and accuracy are not matters of luck; they may be developed by constant practice with a partner using a rubber knife.

The arm-locks and wrist-holds especially should be practiced against a left-hand attack.

120

Illus. 109: The arm-lock and throw fells the opponent.

Illus. 110: Beginning the swinging arm-lock.

Swinging Arm-Lock and Twist-Throw

This throw is another favorite with government agents; it is a technique requiring speedy execution.

Grasp your opponent's wrist with both hands. Swing his arm quickly up and over your head, as you pivot to the left on your left foot (see page 123). Continued twisting pressure on his wrist will force your opponent's body to bend forward and down. Further twisting will bring him to the ground.

Be very careful in practicing this with your partner. Violent twisting will cause considerable pain, and possible injury to his arm.

Like the previous arm-lock, this too may be used as a defense against knife attack. In this case it is useful against an underhand

Illus. 111: Start the swing up.

Illus. 112: Bring opponent's arm way up.

123

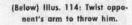

(Left) Illus. 113: Pivot around in the swinging arm-lock.

(Below) Illus. 114: Twist opponent's arm to throw him.

thrust, which must first be parried to the side or met with slashing karate blows to the forearm and elbow joint.

124

PART II—RELEASES

A stronger adversary may attempt to restrain, pull, or push you by using a tight grip on either or both of your wrists. Releases from wrist-holds are easy to master, and should be learned early. You would do well to practice these until your response is automatic. Releases are good when you're in no real danger, and you don't want to take a chance of hurting your opponent by throwing him.

Release from Wrist-Hold on Both Hands

Twist your hands outward, *always in the direction of your opponent's thumb.*

Illus. 115: Twist hands outward to break wrist-hold.

Illus. 116: The wrist-hold is broken.

If your opponent is considerably stronger, use the following mock-resistance technique: Start to push your hands outward toward your opponent's fingers, as if trying to pull away. Your opponent will resist your movement, and try to pull you in closer. Then snap your hands quickly in and upwards, twisting toward your opponent's thumbs. This will break the hold.

Release from Single-Hand-Hold on One Hand

This is the easiest release, and uses the same basic technique as above. Twist your hand away in direction of your opponent's thumb. This is a basic leverage technique, well known to lifeguards, who must be able to release themselves quickly from the desperate, clinging grip of panicky swimmers.

(Above) Illus. 117: Twist toward opponent's thumb in this hold.

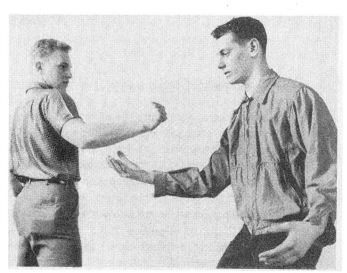

Illus. 118: The release comes easily.

127

Illus. 119: The hold is tight.

Release from Two-Hand-Hold on One Wrist

In this situation your opponent has one of your wrists captured with a combination overhand-underhand grip. Reach down between his hands to grasp your own hand, without interlocking your fingers. Bend your knees, keep your elbows tucked in close to body. Straighten your knees with a snap; use your arm, shoulder, and body strength to bring your clasped hands up and out quickly and powerfully, in an uppercut motion. (With luck, you may connect.)

Again, if your opponent is too strong for this, use the mock-resistance technique. Instead of pulling away, use your free hand to grasp your own hand, and push down until your opponent begins to pull up. Then help him: pull up harder and faster than he expects.

128

(Above) Illus. 120: Grasp your own hand.

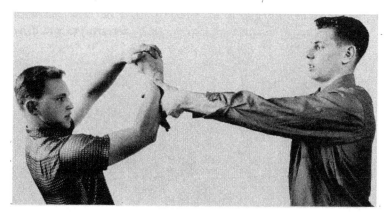

Illus. 121: An uppercut breaks the hold.

129

Illus. 122: The choke-hold.

Release from Choke-Holds

Defenses against choke-holds are even more important than wrist-hold releases, and should be learned and mastered early. A choke is always a frightening hold. The automatic response will minimize the danger of becoming panicky in this situation.

This is the defense against the choke-hold from the front: Clasp your hands together as in previous defense. Your arms should not be held straight. Your elbows should be bent and arms spread enough to contact your opponent's forearms as you drive up hard with your arms.

Illus. 123: Clasped hands achieve release.

130

Against the choke from behind, the best defense is a scraping kick to the shins. Never try to pull forward from a choke from behind. If necessary, throw yourself backward, falling on top of your opponent or butting his face with the back of your head. These measures are as extreme as they sound; the choke from behind requires extreme action. Do not attempt to practice these techniques. They are employed only in actual self-defense situations.

Illus. 124: A scraping kick to the shins is the best defense against the choke from behind.

131

11. Serious Business

Many books on self-defense describe a number of pretty maneuvers designed to protect you from knife attacks and gun threats, and teach you how to disarm your opponent. We have already considered two such techniques in the section on arm-locks.

It is true that you can develop speed and power and accuracy. It is true that you might, with luck and constant practice, defend yourself against a weapon attack, and even disarm and subdue your opponent.

There is another possibility, however: you might not. It is only in the movies that the good guy always wins.

If you meet someone who is armed, *don't play hero*. You should be more interested in staying alive than in saving your money or getting a medal. How you react will depend on the kind of threat; but the following suggestions are based on the assumption that your main purpose in life is to stay around and enjoy it.

First: Do anything you can to avoid getting hurt. It may mean running away from a man with a knife; it may mean handing your wallet over to a man with a gun. If you can avoid danger and injury by giving in—then give in.

Second: If the assailant is not interested in your money or valuables, and you have no chance to escape, then you would be justified in using any technique, and all your physical power, to defend yourself.

Defense against a Knife Attack

Close contact with an opponent wielding a gun, knife, or club, then, should be considered a desperate last resort. If you must defend yourself, use your feet first. It is better to kick out at a man holding a knife or broken bottle than to attempt a defense with your bare hands. You can deliver more power with your feet; the points of your shoes and your heels can be deadly weapons. Even a boy or girl has enough kicking power to splinter a knee-cap or break a leg.

Violent methods? Of course; there is no way around them. An opponent armed with a knife, broken bottle, or club must be considered deadly. He may be a killer, a lunatic, a violent drunk, a member of a cold-blooded or vicious street gang, a crazed and desperate drug-addict—or a combination of any of those. Your obligation is to protect and defend yourself, and any friend or loved one with you.

Defense against a Gun

If you are confronted by an assailant carrying a gun, and the intent is clearly robbery, *take no chances*. It is better to lose 100% of your money than take a 1% chance of losing your life. Further, you might endanger the lives of others.

If intent is *not* robbery: See section on street-fighting defense that follows.

Common Sense in Self-Defense

On this subject, there happens to be an old Chinese saying: "Don't shoot a sparrow with a cannon." If you're just fooling around with another good-natured guy, you certainly wouldn't

133

want to use a painful hold or a dangerous judo throw. But as a beginning self-defense expert, you have an even more serious obligation as a gentleman and as a person of honor. Self-defense training arms you with knowledge that can be dangerous. It is a weapon, but it is not enough to say that the weapon should be used only for defense. We must say further that it is up to you to gauge the seriousness of the situation, and to use just enough of your technique to gain control.

Never attempt a throw that can inflict serious injury if a restraining hold is all that is necessary. Never kick, chop, or slash except in the most extreme and threatening circumstances.

It is not always easy to decide on the spur of the moment just what is called for. And of course it is more difficult for the beginner than for the expert, since the beginner's experience and knowledge of a variety of techniques are limited. There is really only one sound answer: Try to continue learning. Practice whenever you can. Join a judo club, if possible. Sport judo can be a wonderful, lifelong hobby.

The more you learn, and the more skillful you become, the more confident you will be of your physical adequacy and your ability to defend yourself. The more capable you will be, too, of using the right technique at the right time.

It is not easy to have compassion for a wise guy or a blustering bully, but remember that he is almost sure to be an insecure person, with far less courage and substance than you or the average person. Don't let him push you around; don't baby him; and if you must parry or throw a punch, do it without hesitation. But it probably won't be necessary to injure him, either. Try to use control, and keep your wits about you. Depend upon it: the bully will back down from a show of confidence and ability.

Street-Fighting Defense

We have granted the wisdom of the ancient Chinese, and acknowledged that it is not necessary to shoot a sparrow with a cannon. But one of the laws of quotesmanship is that for every ancient proverb, there is an equal and opposite ancient proverb. So we ask: who ever heard of a street-fight in a rice paddy? This provocative question brings us round to a solid American proverb: you can't stop a lion with a B-B gun.

If you are ever confronted by members of a vicious street gang, or experienced "dirty fighters," you must realize that there is no longer a question of which techniques to use or not to use. You cannot afford to assume that you are dealing with regular bullies. Certain kinds of people actually thrive on physical violence of the lowest and dirtiest sort. Further, they may be armed with switchblades, home-made blackjacks, "zip-guns," or lengths of metal pipe.

You would be foolish to come into close contact with such a gang if you can possibly avoid it. They may not be after your money or valuables, but simply "out for kicks"—violent physical ones. If you are a good runner and can get away by running, then *this is the time to run*. It is not the time to be a hero. Ignore remarks and insults; if you are not surrounded, just keep walking fast. If you can scare off a threatening gang by shouting for help, then do that.

The following remarks apply only if you are surrounded and actually threatened with direct attack:

In the section on defense against knife attack, we said it was better to kick out than try to get close to your adversary. Kicking may be considered a "dirty" method of fighting, but it is also a very effective method, and this is the time to use it. You cannot use lollipop techniques in a critical self-defense situation.

Actually, kicking in self-defense is a highly developed art which originated in France, and is known as *savate*. Books have been written on that method alone; it takes practice to master all the

135

forms. But basically savate is kicking, and you can do it with your heel, toe, sides, and bottom of your foot from different striking positions. You already know that you can deliver a great deal more striking power with your feet and legs than with your arms. However, remember that care must be taken to keep your weight and the center of balance over your supporting foot, while striking out with the other. Bend your supporting knee for better balance, and your body can usually be bent and crouched away from your opponent.

A kick at the knee-cap, for example, is not delivered like a football kick, toes forward, but like a push. (See illustration.)

Illus. 125: A savate kick to the knee. Keep your balance over your supporting leg.

The French method of savate is also incorporated in the Oriental karate, and partly in jiu-jitsu. For taming the bully, controlling the annoying show-off, and in most other self-defense situations, you will not need to resort to kicking. When the circumstances are critical, however, its value should be acknowledged, and then you should use the kick without hesitating.

GIVE A YELL!

You've heard the old football cheer: "Give a yell! Give a yell! Give a good substantial yell!" In a fight, too, yelling makes good substantial sense, because we know now that it adds more than spirit. Yelling can make you stronger!

Sound crazy? It's true. Scientists who have studied the phenomenon of yelling have found that it actually helps you muster more muscle strength than you think you have. Most people don't use their full strength. Shouting and general noise-making can make you stronger by 15 or 20 per cent. (Lifting a heavy box, for example, will be easier if you grunt and groan while you're lifting.)

In a fight, yelling can have a tremendous effect. It's hard to measure, of course, but it could mean the difference between winning and losing. Self-defense experts, fighters, and warriors have known about this for a long time. Think of the Indian warcries, the whooping and yelling; think of the shouting in a cavalry charge.

Shouting not only increases your own physical strength and confidence—it also frightens your opponent. It can paralyze him with fear. In World War II, the Japanese came charging across the battlefields yelling "Banzai!" As small as they were, they gained a reputation for being fighting madmen.

Shouting, in karate, is sometimes called the "ki-ya yell." *What* you yell doesn't matter, as long as you make plenty of noise.

So, if you must attack—do it with a yell! The wilder and louder the better! Scream! Twist your face! Sound off! Put on a good act —it can give you the upper hand.

After all this violent activity, our little book comes crunching to a close. Needless to say, I hope you will never have to use the techniques described in this last chapter.

If you think of self-defense training as a sport activity, and don't worry too much about meeting with danger, I think you will find it a most enjoyable form of athletics—gymnastics, if you will, with a useful purpose. If you are working on weight-lifting and body-building, this will keep you limber.

No matter which exercises you choose, I think you will find that body-building is a pleasant, healthy and satisfying way to keep in good physical shape. Work on these two activities together, and you'll be unbeatable. Along with your new-found muscles and self-defense skill, your self-confidence will shoot up quickly.

Remember: just *reading* this book will not make you an expert. You can't get anywhere in body-building or self-defense without regular practice. You have to get the feel of the throws, understand balance, learn to move fast.

Think of how many times you've said to yourself, "I'm going to start a regular program soon." "Soon" is now. Now is the time to begin your physical training. You can have the kind of body you've always day-dreamed about. You can have the skill and confidence of the self-defense expert. You can; there's no question about it.

All you have to do is start now.

Index

EVERYDAY HANDBOOKS (Continued)

Everyday Handbooks (#201-300) are self-teaching books on academic subjects, skills, and hobbies. The majority of these books sell for $1.00 to $1.95. Many are available in cloth bindings at a higher price.

(This list begins inside the front cover.)

CPSIA information can be obtained
at www.ICGtesting.com
Printed in the USA
BVHW041252101221
623735BV00009B/280

9 781014 915801